Online Legal Research

A Guide to Accompany

2002
Business Law and Legal Environment Texts
by

Roger LeRoy Miller
Gaylord A. Jentz
Frank B. Cross

Guide prepared by

Roger LeRoy Miller
Institute for University Studies
Arlington, Texas

William Eric Hollowell
Member of
    U. S. Supreme Court
    Minnesota State Bar
    Florida State Bar

WEST

THOMSON LEARNING ™

Australia · Canada · Mexico · Singapore · Spain · United Kingdom · United States

Online Legal Research Guide, 2002 Edition
A Guide to Accompany 2002 Business Law and Legal Environment Texts by Roger LeRoy Miller, Gaylord A. Jentz, and Frank B. Cross

Vice President/Team Director
Jack Calhoun

Senior Acquisitions Editor
Rob Dewey

Senior Developmental Editor
Jan Lamar

Marketing Manager
Nicole Moore

Production Editors
Bill Stryker and Ann Borman

Manufacturing Coordinator
Charlene Taylor

Printer
Quebecor Dubuque

Printed in the United States
1 2 3 4 02 01 00 99

For more information contact West Legal Studies in Business, 5101 Madison Road, Cincinnati, Ohio 45227. Or you can visit our Internet site at http://www.westbuslaw.com

ISBN: 0-324-11675-6

This book is printed on acid-free paper.

Preface

As you will discover when you read the 2002 editions of the business law and legal environment texts written by Roger LeRoy Miller, Gaylord A. Jentz, and Frank B. Cross, the law changes relatively slowly. The same used to be said about how to find the law, or, otherwise stated, about how to do legal research. As we begin the twenty-first century, nothing could be further from the truth, for those looking for information about the legal environment of business have a whole new world of research resources, literally at their fingertips. The amount of new resources coming online is changing every day and so, too, is the speed at which such legal resources can be accessed.

In this booklet that we have prepared to accompany all of the 2002 editions of the texts by Roger LeRoy Miller, Gaylord Jentz, and Frank B. Cross, we provide you with much basic information about how to find almost anything related to law on the Internet. You will notice in your text that whenever possible, we provide a Web address for court cases. Nevertheless, there are many other aspects of the law that you can obtain on the Internet. We hope that this book will help you feel comfortable moving around the Web as you seek out useful legal information.

Remember that you should always be accessing the specific Web site for your text, which is given in the preface of each text written by Roger LeRoy Miller, Gaylord A. Jentz, and Frank B. Cross.

There you will find online quizzes for each chapter in your text. You will also find Internet exercises that are referred to at the end of each chapter in you text. Finally, you can easily link to our general business law and legal environment Web site (**www.westbuslaw.com**) where you will find new cases for each business law and legal environment subject, access to WestDoc—a service that provides further case updates—as well as numerous other helpful data for your studies in business law and the legal environment.

We end this preface with a warning: Things change quickly on the Web! As of the printing of this booklet, all Web addresses were working.

R. L. M.
E. W. H.

TABLE OF CONTENTS

INTRODUCTION

In this booklet to accompany all of the 2002 editions of the business law and legal environment texts written by Roger LeRoy Miller, Gaylord A. Jentz, and Frank B. Cross, we will tell you how to think like an online researcher, how to do online research better and faster, and take you to some of the best resources currently available on the Internet. We will define and discuss service providers, browsers, search engines, and other terms that relate to aspects of engaging in research online.

By the time you read this booklet, some of what we say will have changed—the resources on the Internet will have improved, some resources will have been removed, and some will have been added. The general approach to conducting research online will not have changed, however. The first steps will always be to know the object of your research, to determine whether the Internet is the right tool for your project, and to narrow the focus of your search to find exactly the information that you need. If you can master these steps, you will be able to conduct research on the Internet no matter how much it changes.

INTERNET TOOLS

User-friendly software, color monitors and printers, and faster processors have combined with other technological advances to open the Internet to anyone with little computer knowledge. With a few points and clicks, you can get onto, and maneuver around the Internet.

UNIFORM RESOURCE LOCATORS

A uniform resource locator (URL) is an Internet "address." You might think of a URL as an electronic citation. Nearly every resource on the Internet is identified by a URL.

The basic format of a URL is "service://directorypath/filename." For example, **http://westbuslaw.com** is the URL for the West Legal Resources Web site, a resource center for legal environment of business instructors and students using West textbooks. This URL indicates that you use the "http" service to reach the directory path (or here, host computer) **http://westbuslaw.com**. This site provides access to instructor resources, new textbook and learning material releases, and an online catalog and bookstore.

"http" is an abbreviation for **hypertext transfer protocol**. When something on the Internet is a site on the World Wide Web, the first part of its address is "http." Hypertext is a database system by which disparate objects (text, graphics, and so on) can be linked to each other. With hypertext, you can move from one object to another even though their forms are different (for example, text and graphics have different forms). Protocol is the system of formats and rules that enable two computers to communicate. (Because "http://" is part of the URL of every site on the Web, we have omitted it from the rest of the URLs included in this chapter.)

"www" is an abbreviation for World Wide Web. The **World Wide Web**, or simply the Web, is a hypertext-based service through which data are made available on the Internet.

To enter a URL into a browser, usually it is not necessary to type in http and www. The browser will enter these terms automatically. This saves time.

FILE TRANSFER PROTOCOL

File transfer protocol (ftp) is a very basic interface that connects one computer to another to copy files. The files may contain text, graphics, or software. Ftp is the tool with which a computer (called a client) copies the files onto itself or from itself onto the host computer. A host computer set up to receive ftp requests is called a server.

To find files that are available from ftp servers, researchers use an online index called Archie. This index can be found at several Web sites, including ArchiePlex (**www.lerc.nasa.gov/archieplex/**).

WORLD WIDE WEB

The World Wide Web (the Web) is a data service on the Internet. The Web is accessed through a browser (discussed later). The browser's basic user interface is hypertext, which means that communications between computers on the Web are primarily through links and menus (lists of commands).

When most people think of the Internet, they think of the Web. The Web consists primarily of documents, which are referred to as Web pages (sometimes **home pages**) or Web sites. These pages or sites usually contain links in boldface, underlined, or colored text. By selecting or clicking on a link, a user can be transported to other pages or sites, or run other software. From the Web, text, graphics, and software can be downloaded (or selected portions can be cut and pasted into a word processing document on your computer).

For example, the Legal Information Institute at Cornell Law School has one of the best law-related sites on the Internet (see **www.law.cornell.edu/**). By clicking on the links, you can find, for instance, the U.S. Constitution, the U.S. Code, or selected court cases, including the most recent United States Supreme Court decisions, as well as some of the Court's historic decisions.

COMMUNICATION

E-mail facilitates instantaneous communication and provides a convenient way to save and track correspondence. Discussion groups (explained in more detail later in this chapter) provide a forum for discussing legal and professional issues, including legal resources on the Internet.

PUBLIC RELATIONS

Law firms use the Internet for public relations by setting up home pages on the Web. A home page advertises the firm, providing, among other things, information about the firm's practice. Sometimes, a firm will publish through its home page articles on selected legal topics, providing a resource for research.

LEGAL RESEARCH

Legal research is a search for material that indicates how a judge will resolve a certain issue. This is because, in our legal system, judges determine what the law is and how it is applied.

Traditionally, legal research involved using the material available in a law library or conducting a search through a commercial, fee-based computerized database such as Westlaw® (see the discussion of Westlaw® later in this chapter). With the Internet, a third option has emerged. You can undertake legal research online.

What can be found on the Internet includes the following primary sources of law.

- The United States Constitution, U.S. treaties, the Declaration of Independence, and other selected important historical documents.
- United States Supreme Court decisions.
- Decisions issued by the U.S. Courts of Appeals over at least the last two or three years.
- The entire U.S. Code (all federal statutes) see the U.S. House of Representatives Office of the Law Revision Counsel at **uscode.house.gov**.
- The entire Code of Federal Regulations (all federal administrative agency rules). For example, the National Archives and Records Administration at **www.access.gpo.gov/nara/cfr** includes the Code of Federal Regulations.
- Materials focused on specific areas of the law such as intellectual property.
- Sources related to each state's law vary in the depth of their coverage. There is a list of state resources indexed at **wwwsecure.law .cornell.edu/states/listing.html**.
- Foreign law, which can be hard to find in many law libraries, can be found at such sites as the European Union Internet Resources site at **www.lib.berkeley.edu/GSSI/eu.html**.

What is available online in terms of secondary sources of law (comments or explanations by experts on particular topics) also varies. Traditional secondary sources, such as the legal encyclopedias and legal treatises familiar to paralegals and lawyers in their print versions, are generally not available. Other sources are online, however, to help a researcher focus his or her research (see, for example, the resources provided by Nolo Press at **www.nolo.com/**). Many law firms provide background material at their sites (see, for example, the list of publications offered by Hale and Dorr, L.L.P., a Boston law firm, at **www.haledorr.com/ publications.html**).

FACT-BASED RESEARCH

The Internet is very good for peripheral research of all kinds. At this time, the great value of the Internet to all researchers is in the wealth of nonlegal information available. This includes, among other things, library catalogs, phone books, public records, company Web sites, and databases of nonlegal government information. For example, some government agencies plan to put all of their files online, making them instantly available to anyone who needs the information that they contain. (An excellent starting point for federal agency information is the Government Printing Office's GPO Access site at **www.access.gpo.gov**.)

ACCESSING AND NAVIGATING THE INTERNET

The Internet can be compared to an enormous library. Knowing how to get into the library—how to gain access to the information you need—is one of most important parts of any research, and this is true of using the Internet. To get into a library, you need to know where it is and you need to go through the door. To get onto the Internet, you also need to find it and to go there—with a computer and an online service or an Internet service provider.

Once you have access to the information, the next important step is to find your way through the vast number of resources to the right information. In a library, this is done with the help of a card catalog (or the library's computerized catalog). On the Internet, this is done with the help of browsers, guides, directories, and search engines.

GATEWAYS TO THE INTERNET

There are three basic gateways, or methods of access, to the Internet. These methods differ in their cost and their ease of use. The most expensive method is to set up your own gateway, which a large law firm or business organization with money might do. This requires registering a domain name with a registrar accredited by the Internet Corporation for Assigned Names and Numbers (ICANN) (see **www.icann.org**), paying a registration fee, and operating a computer workstation with software connected to a special high-speed phone line. Other techniques are to gain access through commercial online services and Internet service providers.

COMMERCIAL ONLINE SERVICES

Some small businesses and many individuals access the Internet through **commercial online services**, such as America Online (**www.aol.com**). There are also online services, such as Counsel Connect (**www.counsel.net**), designed for legal professionals. Each of these services has its advantages and disadvantages.

The chief advantages of commercial online services in general are that they are designed to be easy to use and to direct you to resources that are likely to meet your needs. The chief disadvantage is that the volume of users often surpasses the ability of a service's equipment to deliver data quickly (or sometimes to deliver it at all) and to provide other support that the service may advertise. Some services may also inhibit or prevent your viewing particular sites otherwise available on the Web.

INTERNET SERVICE PROVIDERS (ISPS)

An **Internet service provider (ISP)** is a service that provides dedicated access to the Internet. There are thousands of ISPs, which are usually the least expensive options for gaining access to the Internet. Most ISPs serve local regions, but there are national ISPs including Microsoft's MSN (**www.msn.com**) and Earthlink (**www.earthlink.com**). A list of thousands of ISPs, organized by area code and country, is available at **thelist.internet.com**. High-speed service is now available in some regions, ranging from fast ISDN access, to even faster DSL and cable systems.

NAVIGATING THE INTERNET

As stated earlier, the Internet is similar to an enormous library, but there is a key difference—the Internet has no centralized, comprehensive card catalog. In place of a card catalog, a researcher uses browsers, guides, directories, and search engines.

BROWSERS

A browser is software that allows a computer to roam the Web. Some commercial online services build browsers into their service. The most popular browsers, however, are Microsoft Explorer (**www.microsoft.com/ie/**) and Netscape Navigator (**www.netscape.com/computing/download/index.html**). These browsers can be used with any Internet service, including DSL and cable.

Improvements and other changes in browser interfaces and capabilities are so rapid and ongoing that almost any discussion of specific features would be outdated before it was published. Although each browser (and each version of each browser) has its own features, all browsers perform the same basic functions. These functions include the ability to set up automatic links (referred to as "Favorites" in Explorer and "Bookmarks" in Netscape) to Internet sites, to access those links easily, and to travel back and forth from resource to resource on the Web. Browsers also make it possible to copy text from Web sites and paste it into a word processing program such as Microsoft Word. With a browser, you can download images, software, and documents to your hard drive. Finally, with a browser you can also search only the document that appears in your window. This last feature is most helpful when the document is long and your time is short.

GUIDES AND DIRECTORIES

The lack of a single, comprehensive catalog to what's available on the Internet has led to hundreds of attempts to survey and map the Web. Lists of Web sites categorized by subject are organized into guides and directories, which can be accessed at Web sites online. These sites provide menus of topics that are usually subdivided into narrower subtopics, which themselves may be subdivided, until a list of URLs is reached. If you are uncertain of which menu to use, directories allow you to run a search of the directory site. Popular examples of online directories include Yahoo (**www.yahoo.com**) and, for legal professionals, FindLaw (**www.findlaw.com**).

SEARCH ENGINES

Next to browsers, the most important tools for conducting research on the Web are the search engines. Search engines include:

- Google (**www.google.com**)
- Raging (**www.raging.com**)
- AltaVista (**altavista.com**)
- Profusion (**www.profusion.com**)
- Excite (**www.excite.com**)
- Lycos Network (**www.hotbot.lycos.com**)
- Infoseek (**www.infoseek.go.com**)
- Ask Jeeves (**www.askjeeves.com**)

A search engine scans the Web and indexes the contents of pages into a database. In contrast with directories, which people compile, a computer generates the results with a search engine. This means that the limits on those results are the researcher's ability to phrase a query within the constraints of the search engine's capabilities.

There are search engines that will search only specific categories of resources. For example, FindLaw, Inc., provides a tool at **www.findlaw.com** that searches only legal resources on the Web. The FindLaw tool can be further limited to search specified databases such as federal government sites.

Search engines vary in the size and scope of searches, in the flexibility of possible queries, and in the presentation of results. For legal research, however, even the best search engine cannot match the results of a search conducted with the internal search engine of a commercial fee-based database such as Lexis® (**www.lexis.com**) or (Westlaw® (**www.westlaw.com**). For example, all search engines have the capability to use connectors, such as "and," "or," and "not." For most search engines, this is the limit of their sophistication. More precise queries can be formulated with Westlaw®, especially for a researcher proficient in its use.

Another difficulty with Web search engines is the quality of the results. In response to a search query, a search engine often lists irrelevant sources. Some of the best search engines will categorize results by, for example, the type of Web site (commercial, educational, personal, and so on) (see, for instance, Northern Light at **www.nlsearch.com**). This can be helpful, but it does not eliminate sites that are irrelevant. Sometimes, these can be eliminated only when a researcher goes to the sites and scrolls through them. Ordinarily, however, the first few hits are likely to be the most useful, and a researcher with experience can often avoid others that are inappropriate.

To get the best result, a researcher must know the features of each search engine and how to focus queries to take advantage of those features most effectively. A capable researcher will also keep abreast of changes to the search engines. Each engine includes tips at its site for searching with it. Also, with practice comes proficiency.

There are two basic kinds of searches: keyword and concept. A keyword search generates Web sources that use the exact terms that the researcher types. A concept search adds sources that use related words. In general, it can be said that the best results are obtained in a search for Web pages that contain very specific terms.

META SEARCH ENGINES

Meta search engines run searches on more than one search engine simultaneously. They are the best tools for searching the most Web space possible. (It should be noted that nothing searches the entire Web, however.) Meta search engines include Copernic (**www.copernic.com**, which requires a free downloadable program), All the Web, All the Time (www.bos2.alltheweb.com), Mamma (**www.Mamma.com**), Metacrawler (**www.metacrawler.com**), and All In One Search (**www.AllOneSearch.com**).

CONDUCTING ONLINE RESEARCH

Considering the variety of information online, it is almost certain that you will find something related to any research you undertake. The ease and speed with which this research can be done is the unique aspect of the Internet.

PLAN AHEAD: ANALYZE THE FACTS AND IDENTIFY THE ISSUES

With research, the key to obtaining successful results is knowing where to start. Knowing where to start requires a knowledge of the research sources available and of the tools that can be used to access those sources. To be most efficient, plan your research steps before going online.

The first step is to know what it is you are seeking. To avoid wasting time, state your objectives clearly and be sure that you understand the goals. To narrow the scope of your research, you may need to know the reason for the research or how the results will be used.

The second step is to determine which sources are most likely to lead you to the desired results. One way to gain a sense of where you want to look is to use a guide book (see, for example, the most recent edition of *The Internet For Dummies*, which is written by John R. Levine and published by IDG Books Worldwide, Inc.). A good guide can point you in the direction of the right Web sites to visit to begin your research, to narrow its focus, or to find exactly what you need. Once these steps are taken, the research can begin.

With any source, you need to balance its utility and convenience against its credibility.

ONLINE RESEARCH STRATEGY

On the Internet, a researcher uses traditional and innovative approaches to research. For example, the use of a search engine is usually the first step in online research. It may be the last resort, however, if posting to a newsgroup (an online bulletin board service) would get a more reliable response from a primary source with less effort on your part than other methods. (Newsgroups are discussed in more detail later.)

STARTING POINTS

Sometimes, a research session begins with one of the online directories or guides discussed earlier in this chapter. For example, if the object of your search is to find a law firm that practices in a specialized area of the law, you could start with Yahoo's "Government" menu (**www.yahoo.com/Government**). This is broken into submenus including one titled "Law," which is further broken down into submenus that include "Firms." Law firm home pages are organized alphabetically and accessible from this submenu. This submenu also includes a list of legal specialty areas through which the pages can be accessed.

A search engine or a meta search engine may be used to compile your own list of Web sites that contain certain key words. A search engine tailored to zero in on specific topical sites may be more useful than either a general search engine or a meta search engine, depending on your research goals. (Search engines geared specifically to legal resources are discussed later.) Keep in mind the limitations of search engines, however. Your search may locate many irrelevant sources and may not spot every site that you would find helpful. Also, different search engines will yield different results. For this reason, it is best to conduct a search by accessing more than one search engine.

From the preliminary results of a general search, you can click on the links to visit the sites and determine which are useful. Many sites include their own links to other sources that you may find helpful. Some Web sites attempt to collect links to all online resources about particular topics. These include directories, which were discussed earlier, as well as other sites such as The Federal Web Locator (**www.infoctr.edu/fwl/**), which provides links to federal offices and agencies. For more experienced researchers, there is Hieros Gamos (**www.hg.org/hgfr.html**), which is an extensive guide to legal information that is available online. Some sites are more eclectic in what they offer (see, for example, the 'Lectric Law Library at **www.lectlaw.com**).

CREATIVE SEARCHING

Information can be collected easily via the Internet. The only limit to what is collected and how it is analyzed is the ability of the researcher. What distinguishes a good researcher from an average researcher is the ability to get hard-to-find or obscure data from hard-to-reach sources that are especially reliable. Backing up a secondary source with hard-to-find primary data is qualitative, comprehensive research.

For example, the Web can be a good source for obtaining background information on people. Imagine that a lawyer is scheduled to question a certain witness. Background information could be useful during the questioning. The witness's past can be investigated on the Web in several ways. A general search can be made to uncover any data that concern the witness. Newsgroups (discussed later in this chapter) can be searched to discover whether the person has said anything in these groups that relates to his or her testimony. Other ways to find people and information about them is discussed later in this chapter.

Interpreting the data in clever ways is another attribute that distinguishes good researchers. Assume that, for example, one of your competitors advertises employment opportunities for engineers with certain skills. To an intelligent researcher, this may indicate a new direction for the competitor's research and development, or a new product line. A competitor's Web links could give you insight to the competitor's operations or indicate a new market for your products. To discover sites that link to your competitor's home page, you could use a feature such as the Advanced Search tool at the Altavista search engine site (**www.altavista.com/**). In that tool, as a search term use **link:<your competitor's home page address>**.

DISCOVERING WHAT RESOURCES ARE AVAILABLE

Despite your best intentions and attempts to pinpoint your research, you may have to approach a project without a clear objective as to what it is that you need to find. Your initial research goal may be to discover the extent of resources available online, with your ultimate goal being to obtain more precise results.

Similar to the popular guides and directories such as Excite (**www.excite.com**), there are less familiar Web pages that contain links to important resources in particular topic areas. These pages often include directory-style menus and search utilities. For example, legal resource search engines, such as CataLaw (see **www.catalaw.com**), are directed to find sites related to legal topics. Remember that these sources often change, and may even disappear, and that new ones can develop overnight.

Many libraries provide access to their catalogs online so that you can determine the availability of particular resources offline (see, for example, the cataloging available on the Web site of the New York Public Library at **catnyp.nypl.org/**). You can search these catalogs over the Internet in the same way that you would search them in the library. This can save the time that a futile trip to the library might cost. You can search the catalogs of your local libraries and those of libraries that are more distant. This allows a researcher to find source material at a distant library that might be delivered to a closer library where the researcher could more conveniently review it.

Another way to find what resources are available is to begin with a listserv list or a newsgroup. These can also be used to update your research.

A **listserv list** (or mailing list) is a list of e-mail addresses of persons who are interested in a particular topic. By placing their names on the list, they agree to receive e-mail from others about the topic. A message sent to the list's address is automatically sent to everyone on the list. Anyone on the list can respond to whoever sent the message. As a researcher, you might post a message that asks for suggestions as to online resources for your research. You can also add your name to the list to receive the mass e-mailings. In some cases, you may be able to browse an archive of messages to see if another researcher has previously called attention to a resource that matches your search. Listserv lists (see **tile.net/listserv**) provide more anonymity than newsgroups.

A **newsgroup** (also known as a **usenet group**) is a forum that resembles a community bulletin board. A newsgroup can be selected by topic. A researcher can post a question or problem (for example, "Does anyone know a good source for what I want to know?") and check back hours or days later for others' responses. A researcher might also browse the newsgroup's archive, although messages are typically stored only for limited periods of time. There are thousands of newsgroups (a few hundred focus on law-related topics). Newsgroup directories can be skimmed at such sites as Liszt (**www.liszt.com/news/**). Newsgroups can be searched with specialized search engines such as Newsville at **www.newsville.com/news/groups/**.

BROWSING THE LINKS

Traveling around on the Internet to see what data are available is known as "surfing the 'Net." Clicking on links within a site to open other Web pages is called "browsing the links." As you browse through the links that could be potentially useful for your research, two problems will become apparent. First, there is a need to keep track of the Web sites you visit. Second, the speed at which your computer browses can sometimes be slow.

A browser "Favorite" (Explorer) or "Bookmark" (Netscape) is an electronic substitute for keeping a book on your desk. With one of these tools, you can create an automatic link to any point on the Web and return to it at any time. For example, you might want to create a Favorite or Bookmark to the site at which you begin your research: a directory, a search engine, or one of the sites that have many links that relate to what you need.

Slow speed can be more of a problem. It may be the result of something, such as an outmoded browser, that you can correct. It is not always so easily overcome, however. It can result from bad phone lines, your service provider's problems, the limits of equipment (yours or someone else's), quirks in the weather, and so on.

Before going online, you may want to take steps to avoid some of the causes of slow speed. For example, to avoid the difficulty of accessing a popular site during its busiest times, you might go online early in the morning or late in the day. You should be aware that if traffic is heavy at a particular site, there could be a mirror site with the same data. A site will note on its home page if a **mirror site** is available. You might also avoid downloading or uploading large files at a site's busy times. It may be possible to increase your speed by selecting the text-only option when you browse. This may be particularly helpful when you use a low-performance computer or modem to access a site that has rich graphics. With some sites, this may not be an option, however, because the graphics may be necessary to navigate the sites.

Narrowing Your Focus

Once you find a Web site that could be useful, you may need to zero in more precisely within that site on specific data.

Many sites contain links to text and graphics within their pages. These links can be browsed to peruse documents within the site. Some sites include internal search utilities with which you can look for specific information within those sites. These utilities compare to an index in a book, except of course you choose the words in the index. Each site's internal utility can be different, but in general, it will work like a search engine. (See, for example, Harvard University's internal search tool at **search.harvard.edu:8765/.**)

Remember your browser also has the ability to search an individual Web page that you are viewing. This can be particularly helpful when scrolling through a document for a bit of information would be tedious and time-consuming. Using your browser's "find" tool, you can search, for example, the text of a specific bill before Congress at the Library of Congress's THOMAS site (**http://thomas.loc.gov**), which contains legislative information. You might also use your find tool to search a company's document in the Electronic Data Gathering, Analysis, and Retrieval (EDGAR) database of the Securities and Exchange Commission (SEC) (**www.sec.gov/edgarhp.htm**). EDGAR is an indexed collection of documents and forms that public companies and others are required to file with the SEC. Or you can access its private sector competitor, FreeEdgar (**www.FreeEdgar.com**).

Evaluating What You Find

After you have found what appears to be exactly what you are looking for, you need to consider its reliability. In evaluating data revealed through a search on the Internet, a researcher applies the same evaluative skills he or she would use to evaluate data found in other, more traditional ways. Because anyone with access to a computer can put anything on the Internet, however, every online source of data needs to be specially considered for its credibility.

Is the source of the information a primary, a secondary, or a tertiary source? Primary sources include experts and persons with firsthand knowledge. For example, the inventor of a product would be a primary source for information about his or her invention. Publicly filed documents are also good primary sources. For example, the legal forms that some companies are required to file with the Securities and Exchange Commission are good primary sources for the information that they contain. Secondary sources include books and periodicals (such as newspapers and magazines), and their online equivalents that contain "secondhand" information. Tertiary sources are any other sources that might be used in research.

A researcher needs to be aware of how old data are and of other factors that could influence its validity. Is the information outdated? Is the source reputable? A reputable source might be an organization that has established itself as an excellent resource in a particular field. A less reputable source might be an individual's own self-serving home page. Was the information placed on the Web by a source that may be biased in a certain way?

In other words, a researcher needs to keep in mind that people can provide information on the Web whether or not they know what they are talking about. People may not even be who they represent themselves to be. When possible, it is best for researchers to find and interpret primary sources for themselves before forming conclusions.

FINDING PEOPLE

Public records are helpful in looking for people, but some records (including most historic records) are not on the Internet. Despite this limitation, Web searches can be cheaper and faster than going to a government office or a library.

BROAD SEARCHES
On the Web, a researcher can run a broad search with a general search engine such as Excite (**www.excite.com**). A researcher might also narrow the focus of a search to, for example, all of the U.S. phone books. There are several phone book Web sites. Each of the sites has its unique features. Some provide e-mail addresses (for example, Yahoo People Search at **http://people.yahoo.com**). Some include business listings (see, for example, BigBook at **www.bigbook.com**). Some can conduct a search with a phone number or an e-mail address to reveal a name and a street address (see, for example, the Internet Address Finder at **www.iaf.net/**). On some sites such as WhoWhere (**www.whowhere.com/**), a search can be based on personal characteristics, such as occupation, school, or affiliation with a certain organization. Some international phone books can also be searched (see, for example, World Pages at **www.worldpages.com**).

NARROW SEARCHES
If something is known about a person, the Web can be a good source for locating him or her. For example, if you are looking for an attorney, you can link to West's

Legal Directory, which is a comprehensive compilation of lawyers in the United States, from **www.westbuslaw.com**. At **www.westbuslaw.com**, from the West Legal Studies Resource Center, use the pull-down menu on the left to get to the "Student Center" link in the Course Support section. When the Student Center page appears, you will fine West's Legal Directory in the bottom right.

To look for a professor at a particular university or an employee at a certain company, the staff directory of the school or business firm may be available, and searchable, online. (See, for example, the directory for the faculty of Yale Law School at **elsinore.cis.yale.edu/lawweb/lawschool/facfp.htm**.)

INVESTIGATING COMPANIES

It is important to remember that sites on the Web can be searched online anonymously (without the awareness of the firm about which information is sought). Because of this anonymity, you may learn of competitive threats and opportunities without alerting your competitors.

FINDING COMPANY NAMES AND ADDRESSES
A researcher can run a search with a phone number to find a company's name and address (for example, see the GTE Superpages at **yp.gte.net/**). Without a phone number, a company's name and address can be found with the help of a directory that searches by industry and state (see the Switchboard.com page at **www.switchboard.com**, for example). A search with such a directory can also help to determine whether a specific firm name is in use anywhere in the United States. You can find out about who owns a domain name by using the free services of Network Solutions (**www.networksolutions.com**). On the top right of its home page, click on WHOIS.

UNCOVERING DETAILED INFORMATION ABOUT PUBLIC COMPANIES
To discover more information than a company name and address, an in-depth search is necessary. A guide to uncovering company information on the Web is located at **www.virtualchase.com/coinfo/index.htm**. You can find out about all publicly held companies at Companies Online (**www.companiesonline.com**). Most companies maintain their own Web sites, which may contain the firm's annual reports, press releases, and price lists. Some companies put their staff directories online.

Information may be available through the sites of government agencies. For example, the Occupational Safety and Health Administration (OSHA) site (**www.osha.gov**) identifies manufacturers whose products have caused injuries or deaths at any time in the last twelve years, and the Consumer Product Safety Commission (CPSC) site lists products that have been recalled (**www.cpsc.gov**). The Securities and Exchange Commission (SEC) regulates public companies and requires them to file documents and forms revealing certain information. The documents include annual reports and proxies, which contain information on directors and stock issues. This material can be accessed through the SEC's Electronic Data Gathering, Analysis, and Retrieval (EDGAR) database at **www.sec.gov/edgarhp.htm**. More up-to-date filings can be found at FreeEdgar (**www.freeedgar.com**).

Some states make their corporate records available online. For links to many states' records offices, see **www.internet-prospector.org/company.html**

Other information about public companies can be found at other free sites and pay sites. In general, the best free sites provide data on the companies and links to the companies' home pages, EDGAR, and other resources, such as news articles. See, for example, the Wall Street Research Network at **www.wsrn.com**. Pay sites sometimes include larger databases with archives of information that may span decades and may cover companies in other countries.

LEARNING ABOUT PRIVATE COMPANIES

Data on private companies is more difficult to find because these firms are not subject to the SEC's disclosure requirements. Much of the information that is available is only what the companies want to reveal. With this limitation in mind, there are a few sites that compile some of the data on private companies, associations, and nonprofit organizations. For example, Hoover's Online at **www.hoovers.com/** provides brief profiles of many companies, with links to other sites, including search engines. For a fee, Hoover's will provide expanded profiles. Dun & Bradstreet provides, at its site, links to approximately one hundred thousand public and private companies (**www.companiesonline.com**).

UPDATING THE RESULTS

Staying current with events in the law, and in other areas that relate to your research, is important. You cannot act on information that you do not have. The speed with which information is distributed via the Internet enables anyone to react quickly to new information. Other media such as television, which are also quick, do not always cover everything you might need, and other sources such as libraries use, at best, fax or mail. Even if all media were equally as fast, data that are online are not always available on other media, even when the source of the information is the same. In addition, during working hours, many persons are not tuned into television or radio.

Once you have determined that the results of your research are as current as possible given the limits of your source, you can confirm whether those results represent the most recent data available by going online. News sites abound on the Internet. There are general, consumer-oriented sites sponsored by such well-known news organizations as CNN (see **www.cnn.com**). There are sites directed at those who may be interested only in updates in specific subjects, such as the law (see, for example, FindLaw Legal News at **www.findlaw.com/**). Corporate press releases—current and archival—can be reviewed at PRNewswire's site (**www.prnewswire.com**). A computer desktop can be set to receive immediate distribution of news (see, for example, the Yahoo news ticker at **www.my.yahoo.com/ticker.html** or other sites such as the Company Sleuth at **www.company.sleuth.com**. Other sources for updating research results include newsgroups (or usenet groups) and listserv lists, both of which were discussed earlier in this chapter.

SOME OF THE BEST LEGAL RESOURCE SITES ON THE INTERNET

As we have said, what is available on the Web changes rapidly. New sites come online. Old favorites disappear. Familiar sites move. URLs change. This section lists sites that a legal professional might find helpful. Many of these sites are not otherwise noted here. Included are references to valuable sites that have been on the Web for some time and have been kept up-to-date. Note, however, that this list is not meant to be exhaustive.

BASIC RESOURCES
Important Web resources for a legal professional include more than law-related sites. As indicated earlier, other important sites can include those of your competitors. Sometimes, however, all that is needed is some basic information: the meaning of a word, the area code for a telephone number, or a local map, for example. Sites with such basic information include the following.

Almanacs and Nonlegal Encyclopedias. These may be found at a site maintained by Information Please at **www.infoplease.com**.

Area codes. See Search.com at **www.555-1212.com/aclookup.html**.

Case Citation Guide. An online version of *The Bluebook: A Uniform System of Citation*, which is compiled by the editors of law reviews at several distinguished law schools, is accessible at **www.law.cornell.edu/citation/citation.table.html**.

Dictionaries. A dictionary is provided at a site titled "WWWebster Dictionary" (Merriam-Webster, Inc.) at **www.m-w.com/netdict.htm**. Sites for legal dictionaries, multiple dictionaries, and specialized dictionaries are mentioned below.

E-mail Addresses. E-mail addresses may be located through the Internet @address.finder at **www.iaf.net/**.

Information about the Internet. Many sites that provide background information about the Internet. These include WhatIs?Com at **www.whatis.com** and the Internet Society (ISOC) at **www.isoc.org/**.

Internet Directories. A half dozen Internet directories, including Yahoo (**www.yahoo.com**) and Infoseek (**www.infoseek.com**), which were mentioned earlier in this chapter, are well known. Other Internet directories include "E-Map: The Electronic Map to the Internet" at **www.e-map.com/**. A site titled "Librarians' Index to the Internet" is at **sunsite.berkeley.edu/internetindex/**. Another useful directory is Webcrawler at **Webcrawler.com/**.

Internet Search Tools. inFind will organize your results by type of Web site—for example, commercial site, non-profit site, and so on—at **www.infind.com**. Northern Light at **www.nlsearch.com/** will also categorize your search results by type of Web site.

Internet Service Providers. To locate an Internet service provider, see the site ISP Finder at **www.ispfinder.com/**. Another source for the names of providers is the "Internet Access Providers Meta-List" at **www.herbison.com/herbison/iap_meta_list.html**. The commercial service America Online can be accessed at **www.aol.com**.

Legal Dictionaries. There is a European law dictionary at http://library.ukc.ac.uk/library/lawlinks/european.html. The 'Lectric Law Library provides a dictionary of legal terms at www.lectlaw.com/d-a.htm. There is a "plain language" legal dictionary titled "WWLIA Legal Dictionary" at www.wwlia.org/diction.htm. West's Law Dictionary can be found at http://www.wld.com/conbus/orans/ .

Library Catalogs. For lists of links to the catalogs of libraries that may be accessed online, consult Yahoo's Library Collection at www.yahoo.com/Reference/Libraries. The Library of Congress offers a collection of links to other libraries' catalogs at lcWeb.loc.gov/z3950/gateway.html. For a list of the catalogs of law libraries that may be available, see Hieros Gamos' "Libraries and Library Catalogs" at www.hg.org/toplibrary.html.

Maps. U.S. Street Maps is a site that provides what its name implies at www.mapblast.com/. Another useful site is the U.S. Geological Surveys "National Mapping Information" at mapping.usgs.gov. See also World Maps at www.lib.utexas.edu/Libs/PCL/Map_collection/Map_collection.html.

Multiple Dictionaries. On-Line Dictionaries includes links to more than 500 dictionaries in over 140 languages at www.yourdictionary.com .

Specialized Dictionaries. One Look at www.onelook.com/ offers an engine that searches hundreds of dictionaries focused on such special topics as business, medicine, science, technology, and the Internet.

Telephone Directories. All U.S. phone books are online at Switchboard at www.switchboard.com. These books are also available at www.555-1212.com. A directory of toll-free numbers can be found at "AT&T Toll-Free Solutions at www.att.com/tollfree/index.html.

Thesauri. The WWWebster Dictionary site, produced by Merriam-Webster, Inc., includes a thesaurus at www.m-w.com/thesaurus.htm *Roget's Thesaurus* is accessible through a couple of URLs, including Web.cs.city.ac.uk/text/roget/thesaurus.html. Try also www.thesaurus.com .

Zip Codes. For zip codes, see the U.S. Postal Service site at **www.usps.gov/ ncsc/lookups/lookup_zip+4.html**.

UNIVERSITY SITES

Many universities, colleges, law schools, and other academic institutions are dedicated to making the Internet and its related technology an essential part of professional research. Their Web sites are often good points from which to start because in general they provide updated material and links to other resources. These sites include the following.

Law-related Starting Points. The Legal Information Institute at Cornell Law School is a good starting place for online legal research. The URL is **www.law.cornell.edu**. This site includes many United States Supreme Court decisions (within hours or days of their release) and links to many other law-related sites and services.

Another good site is the World Wide Web Virtual Law Library maintained by the Indiana University School of Law at **www.law.indiana.edu/v-lib/index.html** . This is a comprehensive, up-to-date, subject index of law-related topics.

LawLists, a site produced at the University of Chicago, is online at **www.lib.uchicago.edu/~llou/lawlists/info.html**. This site contains an extensive listing of law-related discussion groups, including legal listservs.

Meta-Index for Legal Research at Georgia State University College of Law (**gsulaw.gsu.edu/metaindex**) enables a researcher to run a search in several Web sites' internal search tools simultaneously.

WashLaw WEB at **http://washburnlaw.edu/lawlib/resource.htm** is produced by Washburn University. This site includes a comprehensive collection of links to legal resources on the Web.

Northwestern University, at Oyez Oyez Oyez: A Supreme Court Database (**court.it-services.nwu.edu/oyez**), provides digital audio (RealAudio) of the oral arguments in many important United States Supreme Court cases, as well as recordings of some of the announcements of the Court's opinions.

Government Resources Listings. The site of the Documents Center of the University of Michigan Library is a reference point for local, state, federal, foreign, and international law resources on the Web. The URL is **www.lib.umich.edu/ libhome/Documents.center/index.html**. This site is one of the most comprehensive lists of links to government documents on the Web, with descriptions of what is included at each link.

Law-related Discussion Groups. To receive information about new and updated resources related to the law, subscribe to LAWSRC-L by sending an e-mail note to **mailto:listserv@listserv.law.cornell.edu**. In the note, state, "subscribe LAWSRC-L <your name>".

NET-LAWYERS is a discussion group that involves primarily practicing attorneys in how to use the Internet. To subscribe, send a message to **mailto:net-lawyers-request@Webcom.com**. In the message, state, "subscribe NET-LAWYERS <your name>".

Web Site Evaluations. Questions to use when considering the reliability and accuracy of a particular Web site are listed at a site titled "Ten Cs for Evaluating Internet Resources." The URL is **www.uwec.edu/Admin/Library/Guides/tencs.html**

Questions are also listed at "Thinking Critically about World Wide Web Resources" at **www.library.ucla.edu/libraries/college/help/critical/index.htm** .

GOVERNMENT SITES

The government—the federal government, in particular—provides many excellent resources online. Nearly every federal agency has its own Web site. Some of the most useful sites for a paralegal include the following.

Law-related Starting Points. The House of Representatives Library at **www.house.gov** is one of the best government-supported resources of material on the Web. This site contains the full text of pending legislation and congressional testimony. The "Law Library" section contains a wealth of legal resources. The Library of Congress's Thomas site (**thomas.loc.gov**) duplicates some of the House site's materials, but it does not include the "Law Library."

Business and Economic Information. The Web site of the U.S. Department of Commerce, at **www.doc.gov**, contains a wealth of business and economic statistical data and other information. Some of it is available only for a fee. There are links to other government agencies' sites, including the home page of the U.S. Patent and Trademark Office.

Information about Public Companies. The Electronic Data Gathering, Analysis, and Retrieval (EDGAR) database of the Securities and Exchange Commission (SEC) is available at **www.sec.gov/edgarhp.htm**. This database contains public companies' electronic filings of documents and forms that the SEC requires. This is one of the best resources on the Web for information about public companies. Also go to **www.freeedgar.com** .

Government Publications. GPO Access is the title of the Government Printing Office's database containing the full text of the *Code of Federal Regulations*, the *Congressional Record*, the *Federal Register*, all versions of all bills introduced in Congress, the current *Government Manual*, the *United States Code*, and other government publications. The URL is **www.access.gpo.gov/su_docs/db2.html** .

Discussion Group. To learn about new government sources that appear on the Web, subscribe to GOVDOC-L. Send a message to **mailto:listserv@psuvm.psu.edu** or **mailto:listserv@psuvm.bitnet**. The message should read "subscribe GOVDOC-L <your name>".

SITES FOR ASSOCIATIONS AND ORGANIZATIONS
Some online databases that catalog associations, professional organizations, and nonprofit organizations include the following.

Associations. Associations Online includes Web links to more than five hundred associations divided into categories. The address is **www.ipl.org/ref/AON/**.

Yahoo's directory includes a list of professional associations at **www.yahoo.com/Business_and_Economy/Organizations/Professional/**.

Professional Organizations. Professional organizations indexed alphabetically can be found at **www.indiana.edu/~kinsey/professional.html** . Directed specifically at paralegals is the National Federation of Paralegals Legal Resources site at **www.paralegals.org/LegalResources/home.html**.

Nonprofit Organizations. More than one million nonprofit organizations are included in a database maintained by the Internet Nonprofit Center at **www.nonprofits.org/**. This site includes links to the Web pages of many nonprofit organizations.

FREE COMMERCIAL SITES
Commercial sites are Web pages that are maintained or supported by for-profit organizations (as opposed to academic institutions, the government, and nonprofit organizations). Some commercial sites such as Westlaw® charge for their use. These are fee-based, or pay, commercial sites. Other sites pay for themselves with

on-site advertising. These are free commercial sites. Free commercial sites that may be of value to a legal professional include the following.

All-purpose Starting Points. Yahoo organizes, categorizes, and subdivides the most comprehensive list of URLs on the Web. New Web addresses are added the rate of hundreds per day. Yahoo's address is **www.yahoo.com**.

Internet orientation, Internet tools, and Internet guides are the subjects of the Internet Web Text Index at **www.december.com/Web/text/index.html**.

A collection of references to subject guides can be found at the Argus Clearinghouse site at **www.clearinghouse.net/index.html**.

Law-related Starting Points. West Legal Studies Resource Center—is at **www.westbuslaw.com/**. This site includes daily law highlights, an overview of the U.S. court system, study aids for students, links to a law dictionary and a law-yers' directory, and more.

"The Internet Legal Resource Guide" at **www.ilrg.com/** is an index of ap-proximately four thousand law-related Web sites, categorized by topic. The site also includes the "LawRunner: A Legal Research Tool," which is preprogrammed to run your search terms in templates across as many as thirty million Web pages.

The "Internet Tools for Lawyers" can be found at **www.netlawtools.com/research/index.html**. This site is both a guide to research on the Web and a good starting point with links to other online resources.

The sponsors of the "Findlaw" Web site offer links at their site at **www.findlaw.com** to legal resources on the Web that the sponsors find to be particularly useful. These resources include government sites, as well as sites maintained by libraries, law schools, law firms, private companies, and others.

Law-related search engines are linked at "Virtual Legal Search Engines," a site produced by Virtual Search Engines, at **www.virtualfreesites.com/search.legal.html**. This site also includes a number of basic references (dictionaries, for example) and links to search engines for other topics.

"Law Library Resource Xchange" (LLRX) at **www.llrx.com/** provides links to a number of resource sites on the net, ranging from legal research to library products and services. This site, which is maintained by Law Library Resource Xchange, L.L.C., includes timely and updated articles relating to research and li-brary topics.

Thousands of law-related materials and products are available through the 'Lectric Law Library at **www.lectlaw.com**. Most of the information files are not links to other sites but are actually at this site, with plain text and simple graphics and without frames. Most of the larger items are compressed for downloading. Also included are legal forms and a law dictionary.

Media Directory. The American Journalism Review site contains more than eight thousand links to the online pages of newspapers, magazines, and other media, at **www.newslink.org/menu.html**.

Appendix

Evaluating Online Resources

One of the major concerns that many people have about the Internet is also one of its main advantages. Anybody can (and many have!) put up their own information, or home pages on the Web, for everybody to see. Some of the same rules about evaluation of print material also apply to the Internet. This appendix reviews some of the points to consider when applying those rules to Internet resources.

Here are three basic tips to keep in mind. First of all, when you get to a Web site, find out who has created it. If it was created by an institution that you already trust, you can probably trust the information in its Web site. Second, ask yourself why the information is available to you. Commercial Web sites are on the Internet to sell products. Third, be aware that there are some groups who have found the Internet to be a really inexpensive and effective way to promote their point of view, even if it is off-the-wall, pornographic, or just plain wrong.

What Information Is Relevant?

Facts? Opinions? Statistics? Background information? What are you looking for? The first step in evaluating a source is to know exactly what information is relevant to your research. What is the purpose of your search? What is its focus? A good researcher tests resources against the purpose and focus of his or her search.

With a purpose and focus in mind, a researcher can refine his or her search. This is the key to finding information quickly. With only a vague notion of purpose and a couple of general search terms, a researcher will waste much time viewing irrelevant sources. By specifying two or more words that, for example, a Web page must contain, however, a researcher can narrow a search most usefully to links that are more on point. Other Web pages are noise. Most search engines will rank results according to how relevant they appear are to the terms used in the search. Some search engines will further help to refine a search. For instructions, click on their help links.

It is important at this point not to rely on only one search engine or site. The results of the same search conducted through different engines can vary, and it may take several searches before a researcher finds precisely what he or she needs. To discover more about the features of the various search services, go to **www.searchenginewatch.com**. At this commercial site, you can find basic information about how the engines work, and reviews and comparisons of their performance.

Who's Providing the Data?

When you first visit access a source on the Internet, scan it to determine who the author is and what organization is publishing or presenting the information. Some of the newest versions of some browsers can tell you who registered the Web site being viewed. There is also special software available that can supply this and other background information about Web sites.

Next, determine whether a source is primary or secondary. The Internet and the Web are rich in primary sources, but they also abound with secondary sources. The former allow a researcher to make his or her own interpretation and analysis. The latter consist of other persons' analyses. Be aware, that the Internet and the Web are also awash in sources with little or no credibility at all.

How Credible Is the Resource?

Once the source and the date of the data is known, the credibility of the source can be considered. Who specifically put together the resource? Who gathered the information and wrote the particular document? Is he or she qualified to write about the topic? Who is the publisher? Are the writer and the publisher authoritative, or at least reliable? Has the document been copyrighted? Who could be contacted for more information?

How Accurate Is the Information?

Although a source might be otherwise credible, the information that is provided may not be valid. An expert in any field is only as authoritative as he or she is up to date. The date checks are an important step in evaluating accuracy. In other words, are the data timely?

There are other, qualitative questions to ask. Is the presentation of the information without such errors as typographical mistakes, misspellings, and grammatical flaws? Is the presentation easy to follow? The answer to this question involves a look at a source's artistic display (its visual graphics) as well as it electronic organization (its links). Is the information organized so that it can be read easily? Are there charts and other illustrations to keep the presentation lively and the data understandable?

What about the information? Is it complete? Is it comprehensive and detailed enough for the purpose and focus of the research? Are the data concrete or is it vague? Is it plausible? Is it supported by authoritative references to other sources? In other words, is the source more than an opinion? This leads to another important question.

What about Objectivity?

Is the source suspect for any reason? Is it a spoof or a parody? Is it biased? If it is biased, in what ways does this bias show?

For the answers to those questions, consider the answers to these questions: Does the source of the information provide more than one side to an issue? Are the contentions of persons with other points of view acknowledged? Does the editorial tone appear to indicate that the presentation of the information is intended to persuade readers to adhere to a particular viewpoint or come to a certain conclusion? Is there advertising accompanying the content? Is the advertising related to the substance of the data? Does there appear to be a connection between the advertising and the tone of the editorial substance? There is software available that can reduce or eliminate the advertising that accompanies Web sites.

Are the Data Timely?

As another item to check, consider the timeliness of the data. Look for information about the date on which the information was first published. When was it last updated? In this regard, consider whether the work is still in progress, whether it is an ongoing project, and whether it has reached a final point. Are the references that the source credits also up to date? Was there a previous edition of the source? If so, is it acknowledged? Is it available so that it may be compared to the current edition?

For more on evaluating legal resources on the Web, see "The Virtual Chase: A Research Site of Legal Professionals," which can be found at **www.virtualchase.com/quality/index.html**. This site is supported by the law firm of Ballard, Spahr, Andrews & Ingersoll, LLP. Also available as of the time this is being written is a discussion of the accuracy of resources on the Internet at **www.aallnet.org/products/crab/blackman.htm**. This discussion is titled "The Compleat Internet Researcher: Excerpt on the Accuracy of Internet Resources from Josh Blackman's *How to Use the Internet for Legal Research*." Other materials on Internet research are provided at the Web site that includes this discussion. That Web site, **www.aallnet.org/index.asp**, is maintained by the American Association of Law Libraries.

The Internet and the Web offer new opportunities to enrich research. These opportunities have never been available before. The opportunities are in the wealth of the resources. It requires critical thinking skills to evaluate and use these resources effectively. Investing time and energy into learning and applying these skills can have quick and rewarding results. Becoming a critical evaluator of information and the sources of information is fundamental to the skills that researchers, and everyone else, are required to use their whole lives.